MEXICO

MEXICO

Robin Langley Sommer

Photography by Albano Guatti

BISON GROUP

Page 1: Baja California Norte.

Pages 2-3: Teotihuacán, near Mexico City: The Causeway of the Dead.

This page: Cast-net fishing at Altata.

Following pages: The driver of a horse-drawn cab in Guadalajara gestures expansively: *Mira!*—Look!

First published in 1985 by
Bison Books Ltd
Kimbolton House
117A Fulham Road
London SW3 6RL

ISBN 0 86124 251 3

Printed in Hong Kong

Acknowledgments

The author and publisher would like to thank the following people who have helped in the preparation of this book: Richard and Sonja Glassman, who designed it; Thomas G Aylesworth, who edited it; Mary R Raho, who did the photo research.

Photo Credits

All photographs by Albano Guatti, with the following exceptions:
The Stock Market: 23 below (Ted Kaufman); 4-5, 60-61,
    84-85 (Roy Morsch); 24-25 (J Barry O'Rourke); 64 below
    (John Scheiber); 95 below (Joe Standart); 42 left,
    43 right, 50 (Richard Steedman); 44-45, 46-47, 55,
    62 (Luis Villota).

Contents

Foreword

Even the armchair traveler can find something to please and excite him in Mexico, which offers a variety of attractions to rival those of the mythical El Dorado. The cosmopolite will find the ambience of a great European capital along Mexico City's Paseo de la Reforma, with its elegant shops, resplendent monuments and gracious way of life. The world-weary can shed their tyrannical wristwatches and their everyday cares along some 6000 miles of sparkling, sunwashed coastline stretching from Baja California to Cancún, off Yucatán. Those who seek the present in the past can feel a sense of solidarity with human history in the awesome ruins of the great Mesoamerican Indian civilizations—Olmec, Toltec, Mayan and the other high cultures that culminated in the Aztec Empire.

More recent Mexican history bears the indelible imprint of the Spanish Conquest, when cathedrals, missions and spacious plazas sprang up all over the country to unite its diverse people under the Cross and the red-lion standard of Spain—red for blood, some would say. Mexicans are still ambivalent about their cultural debt to the Spanish Empire, but it is embodied in the language, customs and religious beliefs of 90 percent of the people. The synthesis of native and European cultures is still in process, which accounts in part for the dynamism of national life. As an eminent Mexican author has put it, 'Mexico is still in labor,' bringing forth a new people inseparably identified with their multifaceted land of mountains, deserts, jungles, seacoasts, monuments and sprawling, energetic cities.

The Mexican people themselves are one of the country's greatest attractions: hospitable, life-loving, spontaneous and responsive to those who seek to speak their language, however haltingly. Music and art are somehow more exuberant in Mexico, colors bolder and brighter. Vast murals by such artists as Diego Rivera, José Clemente Orozco and Juan O'Gorman are vividly integral parts of the National University and other public buildings in the monumental style that characterizes Mexican architecture. Visitors jaded by today's mass-produced plastic goods and synthetic foods will find that these intruders have made little headway in Mexico, where handicrafts from pottery to silver are objects of art, and a robust cuisine blends the best of the country's ethnic heritage. It is a rare person who fails to find some treasure in Mexico, whether material or spiritual—usually both.

This book seeks to convey some sense of the wonderfully diverse people and places 'south of the border,' where human life and culture have flourished for 80 centuries. It is hoped that it will help dispel some of the lingering stereotypes that portray the Mexican people as an easy-going, sometimes volatile race who alternate between napping under sombreros and riding out on border raids with a smoking pistol in each hand. Mexico is a land to meet on its own generous terms. The reward is a new appreciation for life—*la vida*—as lived from the heart—*el corazón*.

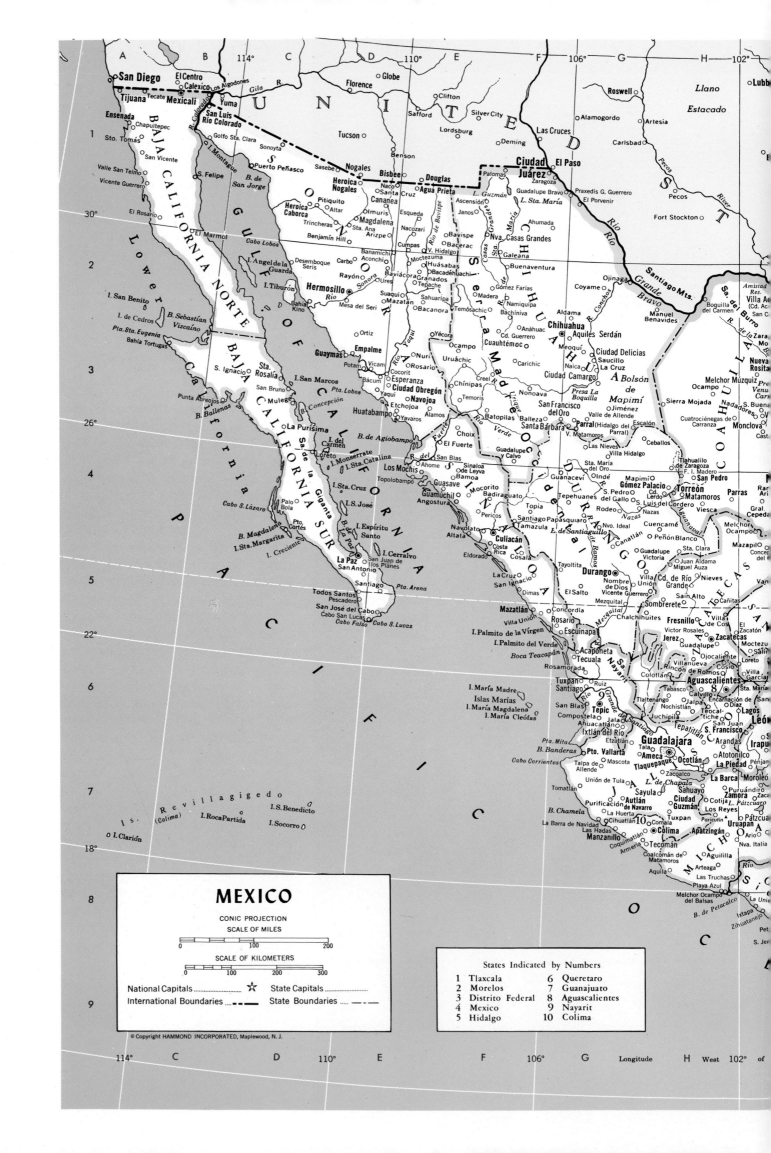

MEXICO

CONIC PROJECTION

SCALE OF MILES

0   100   200

SCALE OF KILOMETERS

0   100   200   300

National Capitals .... ☆   State Capitals ....
International Boundaries .._.._.._   State Boundaries ....._ _ _

© Copyright HAMMOND INCORPORATED, Maplewood, N.J.

States Indicated by Numbers

1 Tlaxcala	6 Queretaro
2 Morelos	7 Guanajuato
3 Distrito Federal	8 Aguascalientes
4 Mexico	9 Nayarit
5 Hidalgo	10 Colima

8

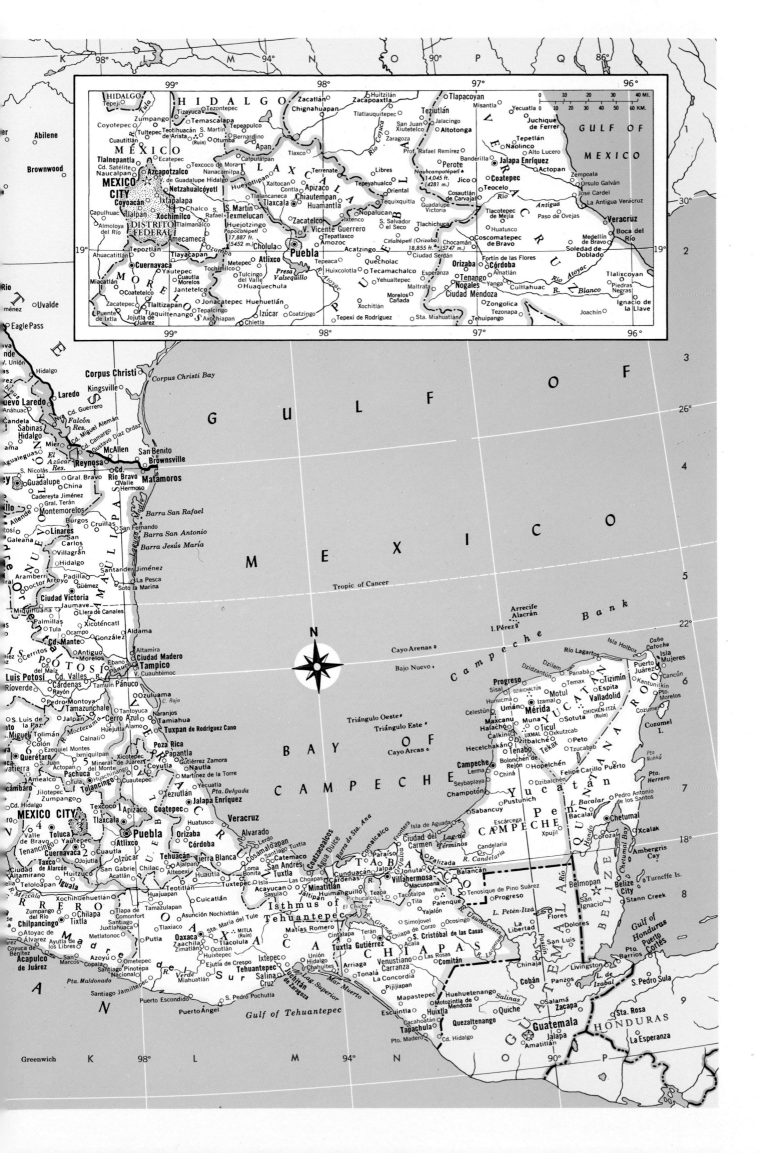

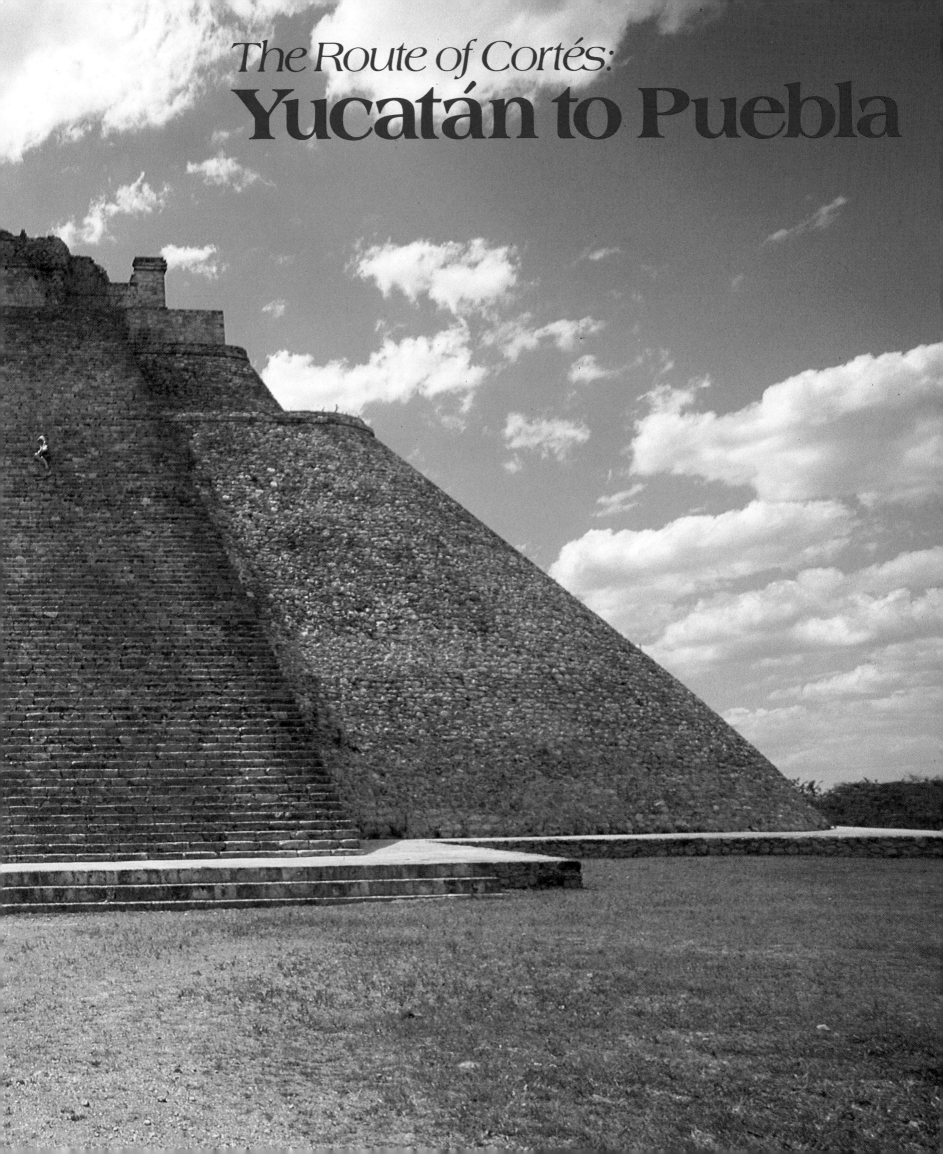

The Route of Cortés:
Yucatán to Puebla

The Route of Cortés:
Yucatán to Puebla

The first Spaniards known to have reached Mexico arrived off the northeastern coast of Yucatán in 1517. The wealth of gold artifacts (taken from the Indians of Tabasco) they brought back to their base in Cuba inspired their financial backer to mount a full-scale expedition. As its leader, he chose one Hernán Cortés, the ambitious son of a poor *hidalgo,* who had settled in Cuba to make his fortune. And so he did, as recorded by his companion Bernal Díaz del Castillo, who accompanied him on his incredible journey into the *terra incognita* of a newly discovered continent.

Cortés sailed his 11 ships up the coast of Yucatan to Tabasco, where the Indians repented of their former friendliness and tried to drive the intruders away. Overwhelmed by Spanish firearms and horses—never seen before in the New World—they directed Cortés to go west in search of the gold he demanded, toward the seat of the Aztec Empire that ruled the land. Soon after coming ashore near present-day Veracruz on Good Friday, 1519, Cortés was greeted by ambassadors of the great Moctezuma II, lord of the Aztecs. They sealed their fate by presenting him with dazzling gifts of gold, turquoise, featherwork and textiles.

The *conquistadores* marched inland with some 550 men, 16 horses and a handful of cannon to take possession of the incredibly rich and diverse land that they would call New Spain. On their way, they found cities greater than they had ever seen before, brooding volcanoes wreathed in clouds, freezing mountain passes, numberless hostile native armies and 'more than 100,000 skulls' piled in the temple square of Xocatlán. Nothing deterred them from their purpose—to pillage the treasures of Moctezuma. In so doing, they helped to forge the country that would be Mexico.

Left: Detail of the facade, Sanctuary of Ocotlán, Tlaxcala, a soaring monument to the Spanish Baroque style.

Previous pages: Pyramid of the Soothsayer, Uxmal, Yucatán.

Above: Another view of the Sanctuary of Ocotlán on its hilltop site. The Franciscans who arrived here in 1524 found skilled and dedicated craftsmen among their Indian converts. The result was a rich and exuberant church architecture that meets one at every turn in Tlaxcala.

Far left: The opulent, Moorish-influenced Church of San Francisco Acatepec, Puebla, decorated with flags for the feast day of its patron saint.

Left: Indian artists created their own vision of Paradise in the church of Santa Maria Tonantzintla in the state of Puebla. Incredibly rich and detailed polychrome carvings characterize the joyful Mexican Churrigueresque style of the eighteenth century.

Opposite: For most Mexicans, religion is not self-conscious, formal, divorced from daily life. *Los santos,* the saints, are *familia,* not untouchables.

Opposite: The state of Veracruz, traversed by Cortés and his men in their drive from the coast to the great Aztec capital on Lake Texcoco.

Right: Quetzal dancers, wearing the traditional crown of ribbons, foil and feathers representing the crest of the quetzal bird. The Toltec-Aztec cult of Quetzalcóatl depicted its god as a plumed serpent.

Center: Vibrant color marks the Mexican fiesta as a day of celebration with flowers, flags and costumes. Everyone turns out in his best for major holidays like the Feast of San Francisco in Cuetzalan, Puebla, a traditional Náhua town where the pictures on this and the following pages were taken.

Bottom right: Many ceremonial dances combine elements of Indian and Christian beliefs.

Below: This celebrant looks dubious about having his picture taken; many Indians believe that the process steals part of one's life force.

Above: Young women of marriageable age take their places before a flowered backdrop to hold court in the traditional way. One of them will be chosen to reign over the fiesta.

Opposite top: A handmade flowered hat sets off the strength and serenity in the face of this Náhua Indian. The Puebla area, between Mexico City and Veracruz, was settled by both Indians and Spaniards after the Conquest and became a commercial crossroads in the sixteenth century.

Right: This colorful festival mask recalls both the European tradition of Mardi Gras and pre-Columbian rites whereby the masked celebrant assumed the persona of a god or demon. Such syncretism is a part of daily life here.

Previous pages: Working-class homes in the state of Tabasco, once largely agricultural, now the center of an oil boom.

Right: A street market south of Tabasco's capital, Villahermosa. Tabasco was rich in cattle and cacao—the chocolate bean—before the oil strikes of the 1970s brought it a new kind of wealth.

Opposite top: Floods are frequent in the state of Tabasco, a flat area bounded by the country's two largest river systems, the Usamacinta and the Grijalva.

Opposite bottom: The island resort of Cancún, just off the northeast tip of the Yucatán Peninsula in the Caribbean Sea. Once accessible only by sea or air, it is now joined to the mainland by a causeway, and new luxury hotels, condominiums and villas are springing up almost everywhere.

Below right: Most Indians of the Yucatán are descended from the Maya; their features replicate those found among the massive ruins at Uxmal and Chichén Itzá.

Below: Watermelons for sale in the streets of Mérida, an important gateway to the Yucatán and the peninsula's largest city.
Following pages: Club Med, Cancún.

Tierra Caliente:
The Hot Land

Tierra Caliente:
The Hot Land

Mexico's narrowest section, the Isthmus of Tehuantepec, effectively isolates Yucatán and the regions south of it from the mainstream of Mexico's development. It is a land of jungles, swamps, seashores, swift rivers and dizzying heights.

The state of Chiapas is inhabited largely by Indian descendants of the Maya. The Chamulas, or highland Indians, are industrious craftsmen whose beribboned hats strike a colorful note in the markets of San Cristóbal de las Casas. More reclusive are the Lacondones—now few in number—who live in the rain forests, still practicing slash-and-burn agriculture and worshipping their ancient Maya gods.

Oaxaca's more temperate climate has made it a popular tourist resort, but its leisurely atmosphere remains unspoiled. Oaxaca City's beautiful colonial buildings recall the days when this entire valley was the private estate of Cortés. The nearby ruins of Monte Albán and Mitla are a monument to the Zapotec and Mixtec builders of pre-Hispanic Mexico.

Tierra Caliente's best-known section is Acapulco, in the state of Guerrero. Mexico's favorite resort attracts jet-setters and would-be hedonists from all over the world to the glittering shores of Acapulco Bay, where expensive hotels and condominiums jostle night clubs and boutiques. On the hills above the shoreline are the palatial villas and pools of the old-money families who holiday here. The region's second most popular resort—once pre-eminent—is Cuernevaca, Morelos, a garden spot that was once Cortés' capital city. A bewildering array of cultures, landscapes and pleasures characterize the region called *Tierra Caliente.*

Left: San Cristóbal de Las Casas, Chiapas.

Previous pages: Wooden crosses 20 to 30 feet high in the Indian cemetery of San Juan Chamula, Chiapas.

Opposite: The colonial church at Oaxaca, birthplace of two leaders of Mexico: Benito Juárez, a full-blooded Zapotec Indian who studied law and achieved the presidency in 1858; and Porfirio Díaz, his one-time protegé, who pulled Mexico into the twentieth century.

Right: The dazzling rococo Rosary Chapel in the Convent of Santo Domingo, Oaxaca, built by the Dominicans between 1547 and 1600; the chapel was added in the eighteenth century. The Dominican Order mediated between Spanish colonists and the Indians, achieving some degree of political unity in what is now the state of Oaxaca.

Above: Part of the vault of the Dominican church at Oaxaca. Both vaults and walls were commissioned to a stucco artist from Puebla in 1659. A tree-and-vine motif wreathes cherubs, saints and heroes of the Dominican Order who represent its whole history in an incredibly rich and intricate design.

Above: Musicians playing at a home in Chenalho, Chiapas.

Below: Chiapas Indians coming to town for market day.

Opposite: An Indian woman in native dress—San Cristóbal de Las Casas.

Above: Industrialization comes to Tabasco.

Below: Mexico's 6000 miles of coastline offer a rich source of food.

Opposite: Panama hats are in great demand in the Hot Land.

Above: Painted facade of the church at Santa Astata, Oaxaca, a typical small town of southern Mexico. This area is visited mainly for its unhurried pace, friendly people and beautiful handcrafts—pottery, jewelry, weaving. Oaxaca has very little night life, in striking contrast to nearby Acapulco.

Right: Children and friends outside their home in Chiapas, which is decorated in the engaging way of Mexican walls everywhere, from the simplest shelter to the most elaborate *palacio*.

Opposite: In the Indian village of Zinacantán, Chiapas, a weaver proudly displays his craftsmanship. Each village has its own distinctive style of dress, by which residents can be identified in neighboring towns.

Left: The massive trunk of this 2000-year-old cypress tree is a favorite stopping place for local children at Santa Maria del Tule, Oaxaca. More than 150 feet in circumference and 130 feet tall, the tree is believed to be the oldest living thing on Earth.

Right: Valladolid, near Merida: A local woman swathed in black hurries by on her daily rounds.

Below: A crude road zigzags along the tree line in mountainous Oaxaca State. Vast areas of Mexico are rugged and sparsely settled, especially in the far north and the Isthmus of Tehuantepec.

Following pages: The Oaxaca Indians have ancient ties to their harsh land that transcend almost all other loyalties. Multiple dialects and strong local bonds make for political fragmentation here, where 2.5 million people are divided into 570 different municipalities.

Above: A luminous night-flying moth is captured by the glare of fluorescent light.

Left: Glamorous, fast-paced Acapulco, Guerrero, is the only part of Mexico that many tourists ever see.

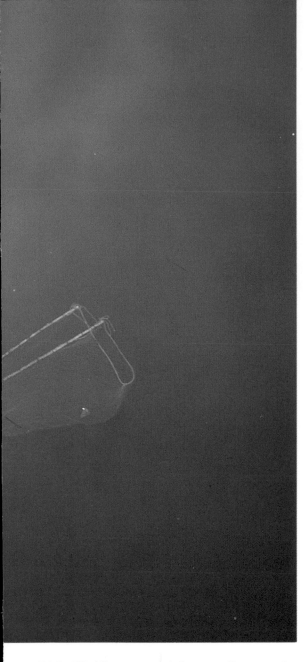

Right: Vividly costumed dancers glitter on the shores of Acapulco Bay, against a backdrop of luxury hotels.

Below: Modern art in Mexico bears the massive imprint of its ancestry (Palenque).

The Capital:
Mexico City

Tenochtitlán, 'place of the wild prickly pear,' was founded by a migratory tribe from northern Mexico in search of a sign that they had reached their promised land. The Mexica-Aztecs found this sign—an eagle on a cactus, devouring a serpent—on a rocky island in the middle of Lake Texcoco, then a huge body of water. There they built the city that became the capital of Mesoamerica's greatest empire in the early fourteenth century.

Slave labor and human sacrifice were the cornerstones of Aztec power; thus Cortés soon found allies among Moctezuma's resentful subject peoples—allies without whom the Spanish Conquest could not have taken place. Luck, too, favored Cortés in the timing of his arrival: 1519 (in the Aztec calendar, *Ce Acatl*, One Reed) was the very year in which the messianic Quetzalcóatl had promised to return to Tenochtitlán. Cortés was seen as fulfilling this prophecy.

Under the Spanish conquerors, human sacrifice ended, but slave labor remained until the mendicant orders, who were advocates for the Indians with the Spanish Crown, curbed the worst excesses induced by the lust for gold, silver and land. Wheeled conveyances and iron tools (formerly unknown in Mesoamerica) changed the landscape of what is now Mexico City. Convents, missions, church towers and government *palacios* rose on the rubble of tombs and temples razed by the conquerors. The Zócalo, that vast civic square in the city's center, is traditionally the site upon which the Aztecs first saw the eagle they sought—as depicted on the Mexican flag.

Insurgency, revolution, civil war, foreign conquest and expulsion—all have left their mark on the ever-growing capital since the early sixteenth century. But Mexico City remains essentially what it has been for 700 years: the head and heart of the nation.

Left: The great civic parade celebrating Mexico's Day of Independence (16 September).

Previous pages: The Paseo de la Reforma at twilight.

Right: Cutting sugar cane in *Merced*, a major street market where vendors have offered their wares since Aztec times. Despite the spread of chain-run supermarkets, some 1600 street markets still provide a large volume of fresh meat and produce for the sprawling capital.

Opposite top: One of Mexico City's 16,000,000 residents, often called *chilangos*, takes shelter from the sun under the traditional sombrero plus space-age 'shades.'

Opposite bottom: Motor tricycle patrolwomen on duty in the Alameda, Mexico's central park, whose green shade and fountains offer a welcome respite from the turbulent traffic of the world's fastest-growing city. The capital employs roughly one-third of the national workforce and two-thirds of the nation's bureaucracy. Urban planners are advising relocation of government facilities to ease the pressure on overburdened systems.

Above: A decorative paperwork design of the kind widely done as a popular handcraft.

Left: The shrine of Our Lady of Guadalupe, the spiritual center of all Mexico, visited by millions of pilgrims annually. Even professed atheists venerate *la Virgencita* (the little Virgin).

Above: Xochimilco, a favorite resort of Sunday pleasure-seekers. In pre-Hispanic days, its floating gardens—on rafts—supplied food for the region.

Previous pages: Mexico City's Hotel Camino Reál (Royal Road).

Left: A detailed view of the Moorish-style dome over the Capilla del Pocito (Church of the Little Well), near the basilica at Guadalupe. The Moorish or *poblano* style imported from Spain featured decorative tilework with geometric designs, as the Muslim faith prohibits images from life.

Opposite: The Zócalo has been Mexico City's civic center since Aztec times, when a vast open square was formed here by the junction of the four causeways that gave access to the shores of Lake Texcoco. Seen here is the Metropolitan Cathedral at the northern end of the square, decorated for a national holiday. Diagonally opposite the Cathedral is the huge National Palace, constructed of red volcanic rock on the site where Moctezuma II built his palace; thus it is the oldest consecutive seat of government in the hemisphere.

Below: An extravagantly Art Nouveau glass dome covers the main lobby of the Gran Hotel de la Ciudad de México. Few cities offer such a wealth of architectural styles in harmonious proximity to one another.

Far right: A stained-glass window inside the Castle of Chapultepec, center, embellished by Maximilian with chandeliers, gilded mirrors, malachite paneling and elaborate terraces from which to view the neighboring cypress forests. The trees were originally planted by Moctezuma II. Today the castle's 2000-acre grounds include a zoo and botanical garden, making 'Grasshopper Hill' a popular resort for picnics and outdoor parties.

Below: A night view of Mexico City's variegated skyline.

Previous pages: The Plaza of Three Cultures, a graphic summation of Mexico's panoramic history. Modern high-rise apartment buildings on the right contrast with the Church of Santiago, built in 1524 by the newly established Spaniards. In the foreground, the remains of the great ceremonial center and pyramid where Cuauhtemoc, the last Aztec emperor, made his final stand against Cortés. The date was 13 August 1521.

Near left: A dividing wall at Las Arboledas, designed by Mexican architect Luis Barragán. Stark slabs of color integrated with the landscape are the hallmark of his innovative work.

Far left: An aerial view of the Paseo de la Reforma, planned by the Emperor Maximilian as a regal thoroughfare between his residence at Chapultepec and the National Palace at the city's center. The photo's lack of sharpness is attributable to smog, which has become a major problem in the capital.

Above: Bullfighting in Mexico City draws up to 50,000 fans to Plaza Mexica, the world's largest bullring, on Sunday afternoons. The formal season, with 'star' matadors pitted against 1000-pound animals—begins in early December and lasts into spring. For the rest of the year, lesser-known matadors and novilleros fight smaller bulls in the name of *machismo*—the ideal of total virility. Its components are bravery, invulnerability and indifference to danger and death.

Left: The National University is a 500-acre complex of soaring steel and glass buildings splashed with vivid murals. The work of such artists as Juan O'Gorman make the National University one of modern Mexico's highest architectural achievements.

Above: History is at home in Mexico City, where the subway station at Piño Suárez was built around an Aztec temple unearthed during subway construction.

Below: Beautiful convents are still a feature of the capital.

Above: Architectural cement blocks surround the crater of an extinct volcano in the city's center.

Opposite: Detail of the stonework at Teotihuacán's Temple of Quetzalcóatl.

Below: The Pyramid of the Sun, Teotihuacán.

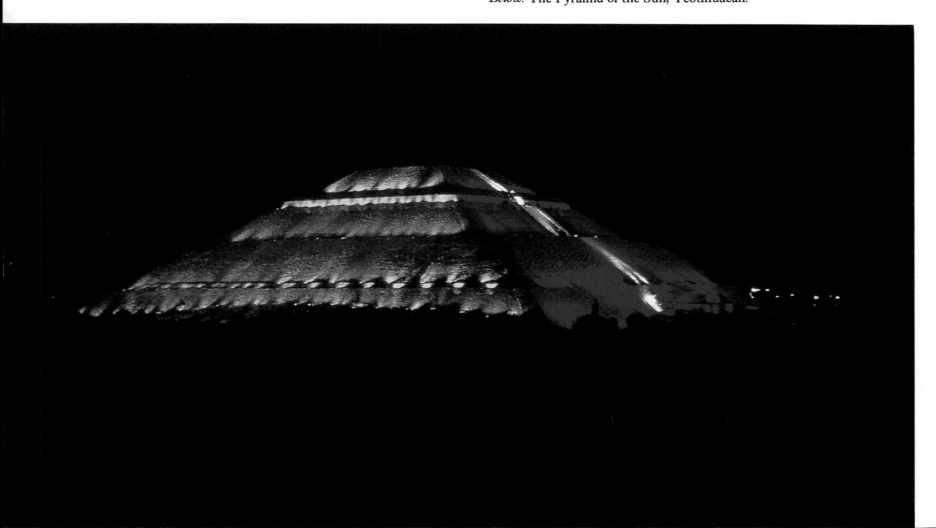

Twelve Central States:
The Heartland

Twelve Central States:
The Heartland

The dozen states that radiate out from the capital area of Mexico, DF (*Distrito Federal*, comparable to Washington, DC, as a governmental entity) show a wealth of contrasts and continuities. Here the Spanish Colonial and pre-Hispanic cultures flowed together in a uniquely fruitful way to create the essential Mexico: Indian, Creole (Spanish who were born in Mexico), and Mestizo—the composite.

Geographically, the region resembles central Spain, with its sere-looking plains, precipitous hills and landlocked valleys. Only Guadalajara, in the state of Jalisco, had a major port on the Pacific—San Blas—which helped make it the second city of New Spain until the great silver strikes, predominantly around Zacatecas, capital of the state of the same name. The mainstays of the region's economy were mining and farming; it was the heartland's silver mines and *haciendas* (some still in operation) that fueled the entire colonial enterprise. Its missionaries, and later their converts, carried the Roman Catholic religion to every part of the country. The insurgency against Spain was conceived here, in Querétaro and Guanajuato. So was resistance to foreign domination by the French and Maximilian.

The state of Hidalgo was another great silver center that helped finance the exploration and settlement of new northern states like Durango and San Luis Potosí. The treasures of Mexico were instrumental in the conquest of Peru and the Philippines as well. To the south, Michoacán, with its capital at Morelia, became a microcosm of the entire region. To this day, the heartland's villages, towns and cities exemplify the living reality of *las tres culturas*—the three cultures that converged here to forge the consciousness of a race.

Left: Colorful Guanajuato climbs its steep hills.

Previous pages: La Valenciana Church, Guanajuato, breathes the spirit of Spanish Colonial times.

Opposite: A field worker swathed in protective scarves against mosquitoes, dust and chemicals appears bound for a fiesta.

Above: Pachuca, Hidalgo: the arches of Mexico's greatest aqueduct, built by a Franciscan friar with no training in engineering and 1200 Indian converts. In the foreground, *agave* plants, long used as a source of fiber, food and strong drink (*pulque* and *tequila*).

Right: Stone warriors (the Atlantes) of the ancient Toltec culture (fl AD 900-1000) gaze serenely over the landscape of Tula, Hidalgo. Their lost city of Tollan is little visited except by local inhabitants who experience, perhaps, a sense of kinship with their past here. After AD 1000, traders and migrators affected a cultural exchange between these central highlands and the Yucatán, where similar figures abound.

Following pages: Dazzlingly lavish use of gold typifies church architecture in colonial Mexico (Tepotzotlán).

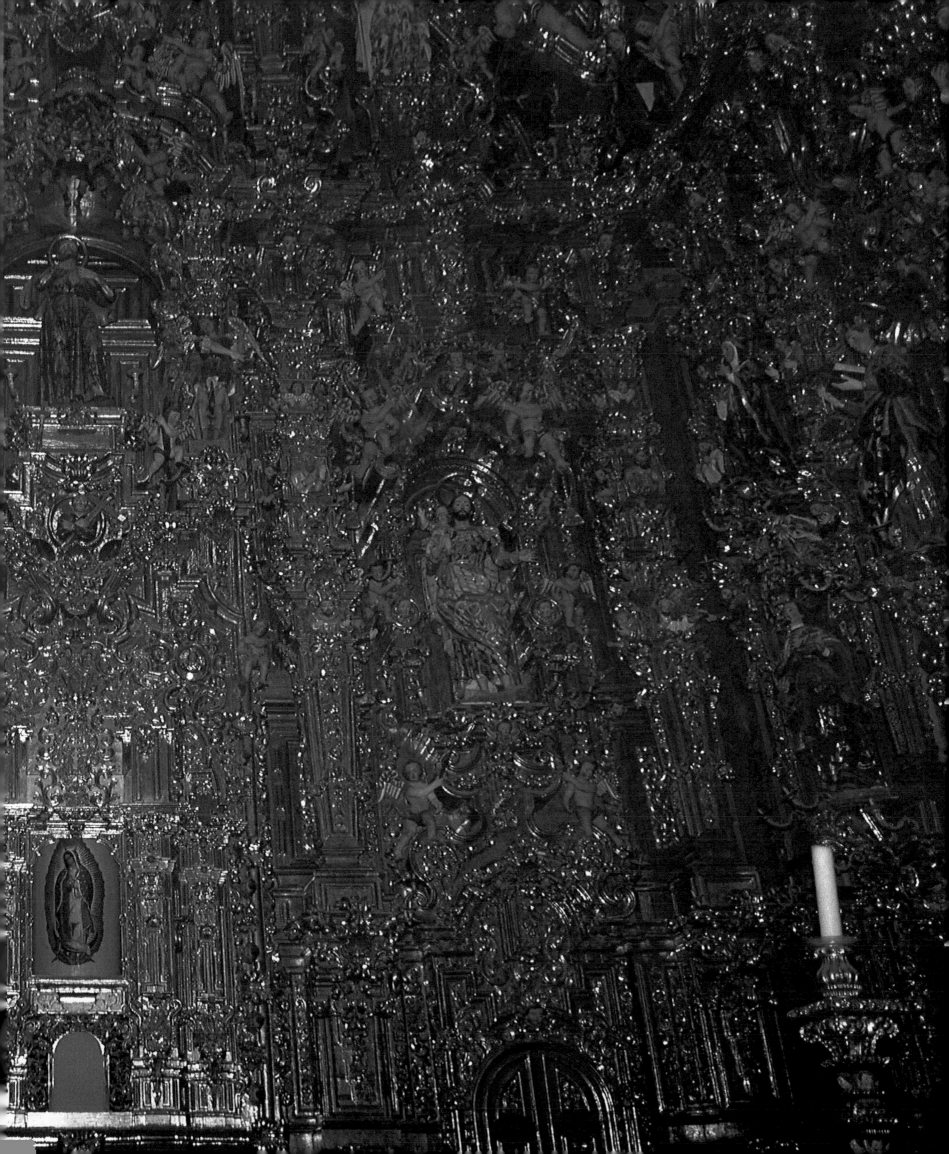

Above: The huge 'open chapel' at Actopan, Hidalgo, its murals fading now, is covered by an impressive vault (*bóveda*) with a span of almost 56 feet.

Left: These sixteenth-century frescoes adorn the stairwell of the former Augustinian monastery at Actopan, now a colonial museum.

Opposite top: The roofline of Guadalajara Cathedral, in the state of Jalisco, testifies to its long period of construction (since 1558), with modifications continuing into the present.

Near right: The Governor's Palace, Guadalajara.

Far right: Interior of the Governor's Palace: this massive mural by José Clemente Orozco depicts Miguel Hidalgo y Costilla, the priest who launched the War of Independence against Spain in 1810.

Above: A working ranch in Zacatecas, whose *charros* (cowboys) still live close to the land. Mexican ranchers and cattlemen were largely responsible for settling most of northern Mexico and the American Southwest.

Above: Conical grain siloes like these on a Santa Monica *hacienda* go back to pre-Hispanic times, but they are less frequently seen since the Revolution of 1910, which broke up many huge land holdings.

Previous pages: Morelia, capital of Michoacán State, is a courtly city that reflects its Old-World heritage.

Opposite top: Morelia Cathedral, constructed of luminous pink stone, was over 100 years in the building. It faces a long arcade of sidewalk cafes on the main plaza, where residents greet the infrequent *turisto* with friendly curiosity.

Opposite bottom: A lumber yard in the State of Durango, astride the rugged Sierra Madre Occidental.

Above: The pioneer spirit of the western high country is captured at the railroad station in La Joya, Durango. The region is characterized by magnificent scenery.

Right: The State of Jalisco is watered by the streams that flow down from central Mexico's mountains to irrigate the plains along both coasts. Its original inhabitants were nomadic hunters and fishermen.

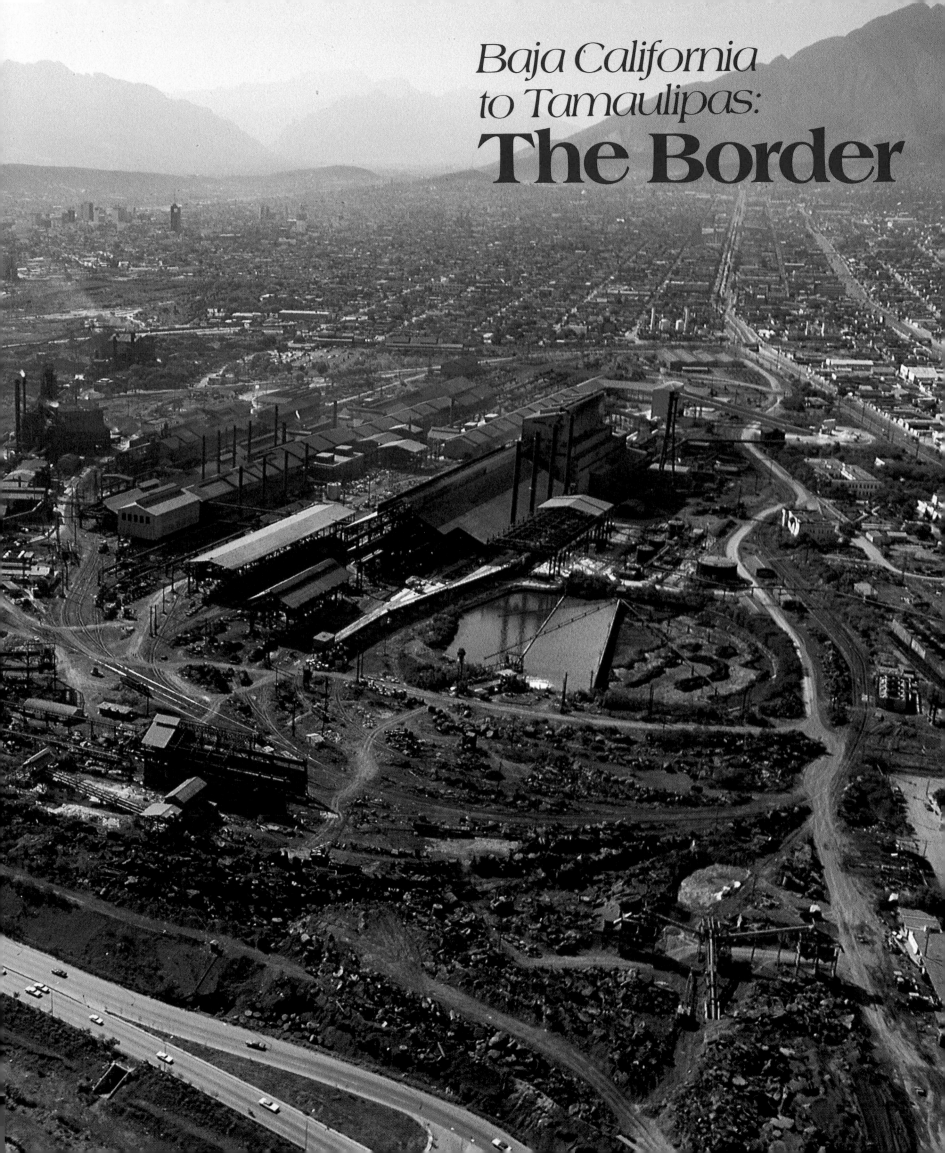

Baja California to Tamaulipas:

The Border

North American travelers to Mexico do well to remember that the country's two largest and richest border states—Texas and California—passed under American control in the mid-nineteenth century after a bitter struggle. This helps explain the common (only half-humorous) Mexican proverb, 'Woe is Mexico! So far from God, so close to the United States.' In fact, the American Southwest was largely settled by Mexican ranchers and cowboys, who exemplified the frontier spirit so widely admired in both countries. In the process, of course, they also helped populate Mexico's northern states of Sonora, Chihuahua, Coahuila, Nuevo León and Tamaulipas, still important agricultural and ranching areas with the help of irrigation.

Baja California, North and South, is perhaps the frontier region best known to travelers. It presents two faces: the wild beauty of a rugged interior slashed by arroyos and crowned by cactus forests, and the seductive pleasures of the Golden Coast, with its miles of isolated beaches, seas teeming with fish, and palm-shaded resorts that have sprung up along the peninsula's eastern side and southern tip. From Tijuana and Mexicali on the US border to San José del Cabo, the whole region has become accessible with the opening of the 1000-mile Trans-peninsular Highway. But beyond the highway, Baja has changed little since its discovery (when it was believed to be a huge island). Colonizers were put off by its difficult terrain, and to this day much of the peninsula remains uncultivated, unmined and virtually unexplored. Cortés visited the area in 1535, and bequeathed his name to the body of water between Baja and the rest of Mexico, but the former Sea of Cortés has become known as the Gulf of California. Four hundred years after Cortés, the most permanent signs of settlement are the chain of fortress-like stone missions constructed by the Jesuits, Dominicans and Franciscans in the early seventeenth century.

Left: Sunset over Mazatlán, on the Golden Coast.

Previous pages: Industrial Monterrey, Nuevo León.

Opposite and above: Mexican faces of the border region.

Right: A Seri Indian musician with his traditional bowed instrument and wooden headdress, crowned by a carved bird (Punta Chueca, Sonora).

Below: The cemetery of the Yaqui Indians at Vicam, Sonora, one of the eight Yaqui pueblos.

Previous pages: A view of the rich farmlands of Sinaloa State (Culiacán area).

Above: A young vendor offers his wares in Sonora, a major agricultural area.

Above: Yaqui Indian comrades in Sonora, whose way of life has been affected by its proximity to the US border.

Below: A ruined mission in Baja California Norte.

Bottom: Guyamas, Sonora, fishing capital of the world and one of the West Coast's most popular resorts.

Previous page: Baja California: a mecca for travelers drawn by pastel deserts, cloud-wreathed peaks and pristine beaches.

Opposite: The colonial church at Real de Catorce, now almost a ghost town.

Above: The State of Sonora is one of the most productive agricultural areas of northern Mexico, as a result of irrigation. The desert areas support large herds of cattle.

Right: Cabo San Lucas, a plush resort area at the end of the great Baja Peninsula. Here pirates once lay in wait for the richly laden Manila galleon, en route to Acapulco, the gateway to the Orient.

Following pages: Mexico—steeped in flowers, faith and the hunger for life that has marked every epoch of its vibrant history.